Malcolm Leach was born in Eastbourne in August 1940. Due to the anticipated invasion by Hitler's army, his mother, a Home Teacher of the Blind, was evacuated with several deaf and blind individuals and him to Gloucestershire. Joined later by his father, a WWI veteran, and older brother, the family remained. He left school at 16 and spent most of his working life with Gloucestershire County Council. In his spare time, he enjoyed mountaineering, walking, DIY, History, and cartoon drawing. He is married and has a daughter, a son, and 5 grandchildren. This is his first-ever publication.

***

The S.C.R.A.P. Book
The (S)tory of (C)anoeing (R)owing (A)nd (P)unting

The application of an old enquiring mind to a subject it knows little about.

Malcolm Leach

THE S. C. R. A. P. BOOK

AUSTIN MACAULEY PUBLISHERS®

LONDON * CAMBRIDGE * NEW YORK * SHARJAH

A CIP catalogue record for this title is available from the British Library.

ISBN 9781035864102 (Paperback)
ISBN 9781035864119 (Hardback)
ISBN 9781035864126 (ePub e-book)

www.austinmacauley.com

First Published 2025
Austin Macauley Publishers Ltd®
1 Canada Square
Canary Wharf
London
E14 5AA

Table of Contents

Introduction

THE ENQUIRING MIND, & —STORY OF ROWING.
Some thoughts of a Senior Citizen.

I have never written a book in my life, and I am 78 years old at the time of starting this. I am finding that the first problem is to find an answer to the question of why I'm doing it at all. I have never done anything adventurous enough to tell others about, never been famous for anything—music, acting, military, politics, sport, you name it—and you can be pretty sure I haven't done it. In fact, I belong to that great mass of people who are spectators to the great and talented and to the wonderful things (sometimes awful) that they achieve. Mind you, without us, their stars would have nothing to shine on.

So what is this all about? I think it stems from the fact that having reached Senior Citizen years, and looking back over those years as one does when the looking forward bit of one's life inevitably gets a lot shorter, something has reawakened that part of my brain that still seeks answers to questions. I have heard people say of a child, "He/she has an Enquiring Mind." It is a silly thing to say because surely any creature with any sort of brain has an Enquiring mind to some degree. That includes all animals, people, and little old me! I have found it quite exciting to realise that after several years when my Enquiring Mind has lain rather dormant, something has triggered a new rush of activity. That trigger was the subject of Rowing (this includes rafting and canoeing and any other means of moving on water except sailing). I hope I can establish the link as we go along.

At this point, I only want to explain that this writing is not autobiographical, for reasons already explained, but it does contain some anecdotes, personal memories, history (as factual as my limited sources of information allow), a few snippets of wisdom (not necessarily my own), and a very great deal of imagination. It is not meant to be a children's book, but I hope it will be read by young people and encourage them to keep on questioning. Finding out about the facts on things is essential, but you will sometimes find questions for which there are no known factual answers. Use your Enquiring Mind faculty and do what I am trying to do in this book. For older people, it is never too late to take a fresh look at things, to use your Enquiring Minds, and for both young and old, hopefully have a lot of fun doing so. This is a book for older people like me who still have quite a lot of child in them.

I have had a bit of trouble in general over what to call this book. I actually started the story at the end, which is where I am at this moment of time, and went back through time to where I have never been. In the course of this journey of my Enquiring Mind, I have come to realise that rowing may well have developed later than canoeing and punting. What this has to become is the Story of Manual Methods of Crossing Water, which as a title, is even more likely to deter anyone from reading it than the one I have chosen. Another possible title that came to my mind was Canoeing, Rowing, And Punting, but it wouldn't have taken long for some bright spark to abbreviate this to The Story of C.R.A.P. This may well have attracted the attention of quite a lot of readers, and I have no doubt that anyone whose Enquiring Mind does not follow the same track as mine will see this to be a most appropriate title. That, however, is not what I want this book to be seen as, so the present title seems to be the best, with plenty of references to canoeing and punting and rafting.

The title is already long and peculiar, but I did want to add "Some thoughts of a senior citizen" to it.

It had occurred to me to call it "The Thoughts of Chairman Mal". Mal is short for Malcolm, which is my name, but I went off the idea for the following reasons:

1. I don't know how many people nowadays will have heard of Mao Zedong and his little red book of thoughts. To a large number of Brits I suspect, China is just the country that makes nearly everything they wear, drive, or fiddle with on their wrists, so my play on words will be largely lost.

2. It has been many years since I was Chairman of anything, and Mao was Chairman of the People's Republic of China. His Thoughts are in a very different league to mine.

3. As at the time of my writing this, Britain is desperate for Chinese investment, so I thought it wiser to avoid any risks of upsetting the People's Republic by attempting to be funny. So I'll stay with the weird title.

From now on, I will use E.M. to indicate The Enquiring Mind, as it is rather a mouthful to keep writing in full.

I am illustrating this work, because often pictures convey ideas more quickly than words. Below is a sample. It really has no bearing on The History of Rowing, and the only connection with the matter of The Enquiring Mind is to give an example of Man's built in, almost instinctive need to investigate a situation, with a view to solving it. This, surely, is classic Enquiring Mind at work stuff, although I have to admit that this illustration only shows the Enquiring Mind at an early stage. The question of finding a solution to this particular situation has nothing to do with rowing, and I will not go on with it.

It wasn't unusual for there to be illustrations in old books; I have a set of Dickens novels which have quite a lot of illustrations. My work is not, of course, a novel, although I hope it can be read as one. I also have books that are all drawings, Heath Robinson, Giles for example, but my book is not one of these either.

So what is it? I would like to think it is about what can be produced by an Enquiring Mind. We must all have heard the expression often used these days "Thinking outside the box". I would like to think that my book is an example of this, although perhaps it would be more accurate to describe it as an example of "thinking outside the books" (history books, that is).

I have some illustrations involving Birds, and they need to speak to one another and to us. I do not speak Bird, and in any case, it is not a written language, so I have to have them communicate in English.

Just an E.M. thought—do all birds understand one another, regardless of the country they live in? In other words, will a Dutch sparrow understand an English sparrow? Perhaps someone could Tweet me about this? Although on second thoughts, it would be a waste of time, as I don't do tweeting or twittering.

The language issue also applies to the animals in some illustrations, and to the Early Men. In no way, do I suggest that English was the language of Early Men. It is safe to say that no one knows what they spoke.

I will also be creating a legend or two. And why not? History is full of legends, and someone at some time must have started them.

Chapter 1
Rowing & Rowing

What is it about Rowing that has spurred me on with this project? Of all the sports in which I have never participated—and there are too many to list here—there is one that, had I entertained this thought 60 years ago, I might well have considered pursuing. That sport is Rowing, and by that, I mean competitive rowing, not merely idling about on boating lakes (though that is demanding enough). I am unsure where the idea originated; after all, it demands skill, strength, stamina, and dedication. I don't recall being particularly gifted in any of these areas as a child, and I have not been burdened by them since. However, had circumstances been different, rowing might have instilled in me the determination to acquire these traits. What do I mean by "If things had been different"? I mean, for instance, that opportunity plays a role. I understand that in life, we must seize opportunities, but they must first be present to be seized. It is also rightly said that we can create opportunities. I realise I am offering excuses, but during my youth, and considering my birthplace, there wasn't much of a rowing culture. I was born in Eastbourne, on 15th August 1940. The Battle of Britain raged over the maternity hospital, and preparations were made on the beaches to actively discourage rowing, especially by Hitler's Armies attempting to land ashore. If they had chosen to arrive in rowing boats, the defences might have been sufficient to repel them. My compulsory evacuation to rural Gloucestershire approximately a month after birth took me to an area some distance from the river. The primary school I attended was closer to the river, but it lacked a rowing club. Besides, the River Severn at its nearest point is considerably wide, and with its high tides and shifting sandbanks, it is unsuitable for competitive rowing.

ROWING EIGHT STUCK ON A RIVER SEVERN SANDBANK.
(OBVIOUSLY HAVING IGNORED THE WARNING GIVEN IN THIS BOOK)

The grammar school I subsequently attended in Gloucester didn't have a rowing club in those days, either. I do remember, for some inexplicable reason, supporting Oxford when it was Boat Race time.

We didn't have a wireless, sorry, radio, until 1949, so it must have been from 1950 onward that we listened to the Boat Race. I should be more precise here and rephrase this to read "listened to the commentary on the Boat Race", otherwise, all one would hear over a wireless would be a whole lot of splashes. Older readers of this may remember the famous commentator named John Snagg who always did the boat race. To this day, I have never really grasped what he meant by the "One out TWO out" and so on.

All that is now past history, of course. It is possible, however, that those happy family gatherings around the crackling wireless every year sowed a tiny seed in my brain which is at last coming to life.

I think I have a small excuse for not becoming a rower. The opportunities are so much greater for today's generation.

I expect every decent-sized pond, lake or river has a rowing club. There are several aspects of rowing that I find intriguing. Take the word itself: Rowing can mean this.

Or this;

Or both'

This particular row could, perhaps, be resolved by having a duelling boat.

Rowing, in its capacity to transport people on water, possesses some rather unique characteristics. For instance, the rower, or rowers, sit with their backs to the direction of travel. This, as you can imagine, can present challenges. In longer boats, especially those of the racing variety, the only solution is to have one person seated at the rear to guide the crew on which way to go. Naturally, that person faces the direction of travel.

Finally, there are two aspects of rowing, particularly in the racing domain, which greatly intrigue me, and for which my Enquiring Mind has not yet found an answer:

1. How is it that a crew can glide so effortlessly across the waters?

But;

2. Stopping seems to be so utterly exhausting.

All these considerations have converged in my mind, convincing me that an in-depth study of this splendid sport and pastime is necessary to broaden our understanding of rowing, as well as canoeing and punting, both historically and in our contemporary world. It is also worth noting that rowing, along with its companion activities of paddling and punting, remains vibrant. These are human pursuits that have endured for thousands of years and are thriving more than ever; rowing can now be faster than ever before. There is certainly food for thought within all of this.

In contemplating this piece of writing, I have come to believe that the oar is as significant an invention as the wheel. Some may argue that an oar is useless on its own, but so is a wheel. Admittedly, an oar achieves little without a boat, but a boat is similarly limited without an oar. Likewise, a wheel is of little utility without at least one other wheel to accompany it (the era of the unicycle has not yet arrived), and something atop the wheels to provide them with purpose.

We may never fully comprehend the evolution of the oar, but it is reasonably certain that it originated from the humble stick. The humble stick, in turn, is presumed to have originated from a tree. Trees, of course, are made of wood (sticks of dynamite and sticks of rock are not to be considered when pondering the origins of oars).

I have read that some of the earliest known boats, in Ancient Egypt, were constructed from papyrus, which my dictionary describes as "A tall aquatic sedge". These boats would have been bound together to float and propelled by poles or rowed. While papyrus may have sufficed for buoyancy, a long piece of it would not have lasted long when used as a pole for punting or as an oar for rowing. It would not have been long before someone discovered that a long piece of wood was more durable and better suited for the task.

So, let the story begin:

Chapter 2
The Enquiring Mind

You may be wondering what E.M. has to do with the History of Rowing. It is because, if you think about it (which is what I hope this book will be encouraging), rowing did not simply come about by early man making a boat or raft. It developed because of the need or desire to cross water, and the idea for a solution as to how to do it. In other words, early man (maybe early woman was also involved) used his/her E.M. I have a theory on how this happened which I will go into later on.

I don't think that anyone can deny that the E.M. is something unique to the human species. It has given us a huge advantage over the animals. They may have E.M.s to some degree, but mostly, I suspect, animals are guided by instinct. Animals can be very intelligent, of course, and adapt to changed circumstances very well. When our Labrador, Charlie, went blind a few years ago, the vet said that a dog will not suffer from any emotional impact from such an event. My (silent) reaction at first was, "how do you know?" unless the Buddhists are right, and the vet was a Labrador in a previous existence, and furthermore, could remember it. However, it soon became clear that the vet was absolutely right. After a few false starts, Charlie simply got on with the business of sniffing his way around and hardly needed a lead on his regular walks. There are reports of Orangutans and Chimpanzees doing clever things with sticks, but I reckon the age of The Planet of the Apes is some way off yet, thank goodness.

It is clear to me that survival in the animal kingdom depends on everything knowing its place and purpose in the Great Scheme of things, accepting that, and not having the will or E.M. capacity to challenge this. They mostly go on instinct. AND WHAT A GOOD JOB THAT IS THE CASE! Just to imagine the chaos if our fellow creatures on this planet discovered E.M.'s. You sometimes hear the saying about a man (or less often a woman) "behaving like an animal". What if suddenly some animals discovered that they could behave like men? Just take three possible scenarios:

1. The worm that turns.

2. The rabbit rouser.

3. And what if Sheepdog trials really were just that?

But these things haven't happened—yet. Perhaps I can sum up the position like this:

Wild animals: Instinct + Parental training = survival.

Domestic animals: Instinct + Parental training, and training by owners = A good life.

Humans: Instinct only = Prison.

Instinct + Parental training + what other people teach us = Status quo.

Instinct + Parental Training + what other people teach us + E. M. = Progress.

I find myself wondering what sort of enquiries an E.M. makes over the course of a lifetime. For a baby, the enquiries will be few and simple to begin with.

Can it go into my mouth? How far can I throw it? If I cry loud enough, will they pay attention to me? As the months go by, the child's E.M. asks even more questions that can be given practical answers; Can I stuff it up my nose as well as my mouth? Can I throw it at my mum/ dad/ sister/ brother/ friend, while still asking if I cry loud enough, will they pay attention to me?

A lot of this is, of course, instinct and curiosity, just the same as in animals. The real fun begins when a child's E.M. comes increasingly into operation. The bit about crying loud enough to attract attention can be something that we take with us all our lives, even into old age. I must keep this in mind. It could be the early signs of an E.M. telling us how we can get what we want.

We have to remember that children are very believing up to quite a few years old. Aristotle apparently said "Give me a boy until he is 7 years old, and I'll show you the man." Is it possible that he meant that with the "right" instruction, brainwashing, in fact, he could produce the sort of man he wanted? Or does it merely mean that he thought he had a special diet to make boys grow up to manhood in 7 years? If brainwashing is what he meant, it is a belief shared by politicians, dictators, and religious fanatics down the ages that they can control us. If they get at us when we are young enough it works for many people, but the E.M. can spoil their plans. Abraham Lincoln is quoted as saying, "You can fool all the people some of the time, you can fool some of the people all the time, but you can never fool all the people all of the time."

You may be wondering what this has to do with the history of rowing, and I admit I am straying a little. I think, however, that since the very first rowing, canoeing, and punting came as the result of someone's E.M. (more details later), it is important to think a lot about mankind's E.M.

To come back to what we tell our children, great care is needed. There is no doubt that we tell our children and grandchildren some pretty tall stories, of which I want to give a couple of examples.

Before I do, however, I want to issue the following warning:

NO CHILD UNDER THE AGE OF 4 SHOULD BE PERMITTED TO READ THE FOLLOWING SECTIONS OF THIS BOOK, IN CASE THEY ARE SO DISILLUSIONED BY WHAT I WANT TO WRITE, THAT THEY SUFFER SEVERE TRAUMATIC REACTIONS NOW OR LATER IN LIFE.

Example 1: Child: Daddy, where do babies come from?
Daddy: Go and ask Mummy.
Child: Mummy, where do babies come from?
Mummy: The stork brings them, dear, and leaves them under a gooseberry bush.

The child will probably believe this for some time, until it gets sex education at school, or its E.M. comes into play. But really, it can only be seen as an untruth. The idea of a Stork delivery service of babies stretches the imagination too far.

In thinking about the stork legend, I asked friends in the Netherlands, Germany, France, and Poland and learned that the same story is told to children in those countries. I have also learned from Google that it is a very ancient legend. It was apparently popularised by a Hans Christian Anderson story called "The Storks." Google says, "German folklore held that storks found babies in caves or marshes and brought them to households in a basket on their backs or held in their beaks."

WHY DO I ALWAYS GET THE 10 POUNDERS?

I am a bit puzzled by the legend seeming to linger on in the UK, because we hardly ever see any storks. I definitely have never seen one in rural Gloucestershire. In spite of this, the population continues to grow. Things are very different on the continent, where storks are so common that special poles are built for them to nest on. I have seen their nests on buildings, and even on the gantry carrying electric cables on a railway line, in the Netherlands.

I did have a rather silly thought that if the Creator or Evolutionary forces had made delivery by Stork the means of bringing children into the world, it would have saved women the pain they have had to bear under existing birth methods since humanity came on the scene. Is it also possible that perceived feelings of class superiority would not have been the same as they so often are under the present system?

Probably not. I expect things would be more like this:

I can't help wondering how such stories actually came into being. There seems little doubt that they go back a long way in time, and show no sign of going away, at least in our society. Maybe it isn't too difficult to imagine, however. A completely fictitious scenario has come into my mind of the sort of historical event that could create a story that mothers in the distant past might have come to tell their children when asked the old question "where do babies come from?"

I have to say at this point that this is just an example of my own E.M. going off on a tangent that has nothing to do with rowing, but as I have written at the beginning of this book, we all at some point come up against questions that can have no known answers, and then we can use our E.M. faculty to work out something.

For my theoretical example of how a myth or legend around the origins of Man could have developed, I want to take us back to Ancient Egypt. I feel this is a fairly safe place to make up this story. There are, after all, no Ancient Egyptians left to be upset by it, and I'll take the risk that none of the writings on the Ancient Egyptian ruins dealt with the question of what parents told their enquiring children.

So to begin. The Bible tells us that Moses had been brought up in Egyptian high society, but eventually saw the plight of his own people, and led them out of bondage in Egypt, thus depriving the Egyptians of their labour force. Pharaoh was angry, and sent his army after them, but it was washed away in the Red Sea. The Bible tells us all that happened to Moses and the Israelites, but not much about what happened afterwards in Egypt. This therefore, is our place for a bit of imaginative thinking, leading to a story that Ancient Egyptians could have told their children if, of course, like so many of us today, they felt that telling the truth about conception and birth was either too advanced for the kiddies to understand, or too embarrassing for parents to tell.

Just as there would be today after a national disaster, there would almost certainly have been a not very public inquiry into how the whole Army was lost. As doubtless Pharaoh could do no wrong, blame would have been put on others. The High Priests would have been challenged as to how the Stars could have been so wrongly read, and the Entrails likewise. They in turn would have passed on the blame to the lesser priests, and somewhere down the line heads would roll, in those days, literally.

So you, too, have had your body cut off.

But inevitably, questions would have been asked even beyond the confines of Pharaoh's Inner Circle, particularly by the ladies. Who was this chap Moses? Wasn't he brought up by one of the daughters of a Pharaoh? Who was his father?

WHAT? HE WAS FOUND AMONG THE REEDS BY THE RIVER?

Is this a place to find sons who could be just as famous as Moses? You can see how it would not have been long before young maidens began searching among the reeds for babies. It is unlikely that they were successful, so they would have been obliged to go back to the usual way of having children. But when those children grew up and asked the inevitable question "Mother," (please note my use of the full word Mother in this, as, in Ancient Egypt, the word "Mummy" has a different meaning) 'Mother, where do babies come from?' The harassed parent may have said, "they are found in the reeds by the river, dear." Well, it's just a thought.

But to come on to our second example of false information we give to our children: The tooth fairy. Child: Daddy, one of my teeth has come out! Daddy: Put it under your pillow and the Tooth Fairy will come tonight, take it away, and leave you some money. We all know what really happens. I have been very surprised, however, to discover from Google that legends around children's teeth exist in many countries throughout the world; some teeth are buried, others thrown in the air and so on. It could be that the fairy version is indeed very ancient, even back to prehistory. Perhaps.

NO, DEAR,
YOU ONLY GET SOMETHING
FROM THE TOOTH FAIRY
FOR ONE OF YOUR
OWN TEETH

I am keeping an open mind about the existence of fairies in general. There will be Cornish people who believe in Pixies, Irish people who believe in Leprechauns, and others everywhere who have a secret belief in the "little" people. I have met an intelligent elderly gentleman who really did believe in fairies. On the basis that I do not think it wise to mock something just because one has not experienced it or understood it, I will leave it at that.

I am extremely sceptical about a fairy specialising in children's teeth, however. There may well be other examples of such stories we tell children. The whole Father Christmas/St Nikolaas saga is a fine example. This is too sensitive a subject to be dealt with here, and the only bearing it could have on the history of rowing is that Sinter Klaas does come to the Netherlands by boat, but these days it's a steamboat anyway. At this point, I think it is safe to let children under 4 resume reading this text.

Having digressed a little in looking at the E.M.s of children, I now want to think about the questions asked by the E.M.s of the rest of us throughout our lives. In the first decade of their lives, the questions are non-stop. As I said earlier, this is when the correct or carefully worded answers are so important. The old adage "little boys/girls should be seen but not heard" is not good enough these days. It is during this period that the "where do babies come from" question comes up.

School days are or should be times of intensive learning, both practical and theoretical, but can, for some young people, peter out into boredom and apathy. In others, their E.M.s slow down because they think they know everything, and it can take a bit of growing up to make them realise that they don't. Unfortunately, some people go through their lives thinking they know everything, but most of us discover sooner or later that we know very little, and the older we get, the more likely it is that we will have forgotten a lot of what we have learned.

Our E.M.s can still ask questions, however, as I hope I can illustrate in this book. The only advice I want to offer before I move away from E.M.s is: Please let us avoid asking ourselves "if only."

Chapter 3
Early Man & Rowing

{Meaning Mankind, & not just men}

We cannot look at the history of rowing without considering the history of the rowers, and the very reasons why they started rowing in the first place. Hence the need to look very thoroughly at the period that is sometimes called prehistory. This must be when the first rowing, rafting, and canoeing got started. The product of Early Man's E.M.

I have read that there were two types of Early Man, Neanderthal, and modern man. There were certain facial and maybe physical differences between them.

My Oxford English Reference Dictionary says Neanderthal man was stocky, with a long low skull, prominent brow ridges, and a jutting face, but not as brutish in appearance as was formerly thought.

It goes on to say that it appears that the Neanderthals may have lived for up to 10,000 years alongside the modern humans who eventually replaced them.

What a pity they did not leave behind any notes for guidance on how to coexist for so long. I'm sure they would be very useful today.

I have read that the Neanderthal gene can still be traced in some people today.

What an amazing thought that the person sitting next to you on the bus or train might be a very distant descendant of Neanderthal Man!

Not that anyone would notice these days anyway.

The mere existence of Neanderthal genes still present today, however, must imply that the 10,000 years of coexistence were more than just periods of amiable conversations about the best locations to find Mammoths. Contact between the two groups was likely not frequent, given their nomadic hunter-gatherer lifestyles, shifting to areas abundant in resources. Nevertheless, there was evidently enough contact for some peaceful social interaction and romantic encounters. I can envision a scenario like this unfolding:

Early Man. Continued.

From that point on, things simply must have proceeded in a fairly natural way whenever Neanderthals and our more immediate ancestors met up, spanning about 10,000 years.

There was undoubtedly social intercourse, as well as the other sort.

MADE FOR ONE ANOTHER

They may have hunted together.

They may have been hunted together.

I think it is logical to assume that running would have started as a necessity for survival and only became a competitive sport much later. However, my EM does make itself a bit of a nuisance by asking: How did it come about that the Early Man lot, from which the majority of us are apparently descended, gained ascendancy over the poor old

Neanderthals? Was it because the Neanderthals were shorter? After all, the Oxford English Reference Dictionary does say this about them. This logically indicates that our lot were taller and therefore had longer legs, enabling them to run faster away from danger. But this could only be a partial explanation because there are plenty of short people who can run as fast, and often faster than tall people. I know this from first-hand experience at school. I was only of average height but was always beaten in athletics by everyone, whether long, short, or tall.

It may have come about because our ancestors were more competitive than the Neanderthals, and the competitive gene, if that is what it is, must be an essential element in all sports, and indeed for survival in the days long ago when there was no time to run about for pleasure or do anything else but look for food, a mate, or wild animals to avoid. I'm thinking of the time when rowing was in its infancy, and rowing hadn't been invented, but the need to "get there first" could have become bred into our genes, again out of necessity.

Rock climbing too probably began in the same way as running, i.e., as an activity born of necessity. This became a sport much later than running.

Different peoples don't coexist for 10,000 years only through being competitive. There must have been the beginnings of more noble feelings, a sense of the value of "fair play," for example, and sentiments such as sympathy for others, and the beginnings of conscience.

At the beginning of this book, I wrote that it is illustrated because often pictures convey ideas more quickly than words, but this drawing may need some clarification in words. It is meant to show an Early Man and a Neanderthal man being chased together by a sabre-toothed tiger. They are racing towards the safety of the cave. In his need to get there first, one pushes the other out of the way, forcing him to try to get away by climbing the cliff. The first man gets into the cave, but then has a conscience and saves his friend after all by distracting the tiger's attention with a bone so that his friend can get into the cave.

At some time in those far-off days, EM's got to work and decided it was necessary to cross water when it was too deep to walk over. Maybe in some cases, it was inspired merely by curiosity. Perhaps it happened like this: Two Early Men were sitting by a river watching a tree trunk floating by. One says, "I wish I could float like that." The second one says, "I wish I could get onto that tree trunk and float across the river."

FIRST   SECOND   THIRD

There could easily have been a third man there, as the always-pragmatic killjoy. They are everywhere, and always have been. I should know, as very often I'm one myself. In this scenario, he would have been muttering about wasting time looking at logs when there was so much hunting and gathering to be done. Ignoring him, the first man dares to get in the water and discovers he can float.

By this time, the log has gone out of sight, and the second man only sees the first man floating. He seized the opportunity, and so swimming and rafting were born. The third man wanders off to go hunting and gathering.

This may seem like a rather crazy explanation, but I would be most interested to hear of any other theories or of ancient diaries written at the time setting out how it really started. It is very likely that in most cases "necessity was the mother of invention" as the old saying goes. The development of rowing, rafting, and canoeing as sports must have come much later.

Chapter 4
Men In Boats

Having just considered how swimming and rafting may have started, it is now time to take our in-depth study to the next stage: that of men in boats. There is plenty of archaeological evidence throughout the world that boats have been in use for many thousands of years. The oldest were mostly dug out of solid tree trunks, but there is an example of a boat made of reeds in the Middle East. It is certain that Early Men would have made early boats out of local materials. I feel safe, however, in saying that no evidence has yet been found to show that Stone Age men ever successfully made any sort of boat out of stone.

A STONE-AGE CANOE

I will go further to say that <u>nobody has ever</u> made a boat out of stone. They have, however, come fairly close to it by making ships out of concrete. There may be some reading this book who have not heard of this, but it is absolutely true. I have seen two with my own eyes. They weren't boats in the true meaning of the word, one being a ship, and the other a barge, but I think it worth mentioning in the context of mankind's ingenuity in finding ways to cross water.

The concrete ship I saw was on the rocks on an island in the outer Hebrides, where it had been for some time. This was in 1967, when I visited that island on a yacht. (Rather oddly, this was a sailing holiday arranged by a rambling association.) The ship was a leftover from WW2, when concrete ships called Liberty ships or Victory ships were made, mostly in the USA, to ease the shortage in cargo vessels being used in the war effort. The barge was a concrete barge used on our inland waterways, also made in WW2, and is, I believe, owned now by The National Waterways Museum in Gloucester Docks. Neither of these was, or is, in any way a rowing boat, of course.

To return to the subject of rowing (or canoeing), I can't help but marvel at the fact that there are quite a number of types of boat in use today in many countries in the world that have changed little over thousands of years in design, from dugout canoes to rafts of reeds, but none perhaps more amazing than the coracle. My sources record that they date from "pre-Roman" times, which covers a long time span, yet they are still being made in Wales, and used for fishing and pleasure boating. I have learned, however, during the limited research that I have done for this book, that there are boats very much like coracles in several other countries. My source of information states: "The coracle is a small, rounded, lightweight boat of the sort traditionally used in Wales, and also in parts of the West Country and in Ireland, particularly the River Boyne, and in Scotland, particularly the River Spey. The word is also used for similar boats found in India, Vietnam, Iraq, and Tibet. The word 'coracle' is an English spelling of the original Welsh cwrwgl, cognate with Irish and Scottish Gaelic currach."

It seems that boats like coracles were around even before the Celts. The information I refer to says: "The oldest instructions yet found for construction of a coracle are contained in precise directions on a 4,000-year-old cuneiform tablet supposedly dictated by the Mesopotamian god Enki to Atra-Hasis on how to build a round "Ark". The tablet is about 2,250 years older than previously discovered accounts of flood myths, none of which contain such details. These instructions depict a vessel that is today known as a quffa, or Iraqi coracle."

How about that! My EM finds this fascinating stuff, even though coracles are not rowing boats. It all points to the fact that paddling about in boats goes back a very long time in history. This cannot be ignored when thinking about the story of rowing. If Noah's Ark was a giant coracle, it must have needed oars rather than paddles.

There will be experts who can understand their design, but to most of us, I suspect a coracle resembles a tub that must surely have a tendency to go round in circles in the water unless expertly handled. I have come up with a theory about the origin of coracles which I would like to share with you.

It could be that the coracle, at least the Welsh variety, was not originally designed as a boat. The climate in those days was probably as wet as it is today, and in the area where it all began, people built their homes a safe distance from the river bank because of erosion. By the way, I am now referring to the Slightly Later Early man, not the Stone Age ones.

As they had to walk some distance to the river, in cold and wet conditions, someone made a small rounded lightweight frame, covered in hides, as protection from the rain while walking to the river to fish, and to sit under when fishing.

Then one day the riverbank collapsed, throwing the fishermen into the river, still in their shelters. To the great relief of the occupants, they floated extremely well.

Furthermore, they noticed an immediate increase in the number of fish caught. This, in hindsight, is very logical. A coracle, as they came to be called, does not disturb the water much, and the fish, looking up through the water at the rounded bottoms (of the coracles, that is, not the men in them), probably mistook them for insects and rushed to the surface to have a look.

For this reason, coracles often work in pairs, drifting with the flow of the river with a net slung between the two of them.

Before I leave the subject of coracles, I just want to make one general observation:

At the time that I am writing this, the world seems to be going through an upsurge in nationalism. One of the ways I think it shows itself, in this country at least, is through more strident claims by politicians and the press that 'We are world leaders in whatever,' or 'Britain leads the world in... whatever.' I would like to think that Wales could rightly claim that it leads the world in coracle making. Having read, however, that there may be similar types of boats made and used in India, Vietnam, Iraq, and Tibet, this is a claim that could be challenged. There are enough international disputes going on at the moment without adding another one.

I reckon; however, it is quite safe for Wales to claim that it leads the U.K. in coracle making (It may of course lead the U.K. in other things as well, but we are only talking about coracles here.)

It would be good if, in this competitive age when every nation wants to be the greatest, it could be truthfully claimed that the first ever boat was made in the U.K. Sadly, this cannot be proved. In fact, most of our early ancestors actually arrived here by boats that, of course, had been invented by others on the other side of the Channel. Thinking of the Channel reminds me that many thousands of years ago, Britain (as it wasn't then) was joined to the continent of Europe by land. I think the joining bit was between us and the Netherlands, as I have seen in a Dutch fishing village many relics of Stone Age human activity such as flint tools that still get dredged up in the nets of boats fishing on the Dogger Bank, which I am sure everyone knows is a large sandbank in the North Sea between the U.K. and the Netherlands. It is often submerged and is very popular with fish.

While the land bridge was in existence, there was free movement of people.

That was spoiled (the first time) when the sea broke through, cutting us off from the mainland except by boat.

This must have been a cataclysmic event, dividing families and tribes, but once the waters had broken and this island was born, our dependency on boats was clearly established.

I don't know if this happened when Stone Age people were about; if it did, then it would not have been long before they found a way of getting across the divide, which was not very wide at first. I think it's safe to say that they did not cross in stone canoes. As we have stated earlier, they may have had coracles, but probably needed something bigger. They obviously needed these for trading, as well as for invasion purposes, but whatever they used to cross the seas to this country must have required an awful lot of rowing.

This leads us, logically, to think about the impact of rowing on the history of this country. Another excuse for the EM to get busy again. I must be honest here and admit that probably most of the boats used to get across the sea to us were sail-assisted. The supporters of sail would put it another way, of course, that our ancestors came in sailing boats which were assisted <u>by oars</u>. We are both right.

Chapter 5
The Impact of Rowing on Britain

When referring to "The impact of rowing on," I don't just mean the loud crunch of keel on shingle, and the harsh shouts of the traders or invaders, but the impact on our history of what they brought with them, and what they did when they got here. It is clear that those who came to these islands so long ago had to row pretty hard to get here. That goes some way to explain why a lot decided not to go back.

So who were those early rowers? We have already established that many Stone Age people were able to walk across, so boating wasn't a big thing for them. Once, however, the sea cut us off from mainland Europe things changed for everyone.

I have to say that I have not tried to find out who was living in this country when the Bronze Age came along, but it is safe to say they were living in the Stone Age. It is funny that the expression "living in the Stone Age" is used to this day to describe anyone who won't adapt to new ideas. We have no idea how our early ancestors responded to incomers using or trying to sell the new stuff and the technology that went with it, and of course, Cornwall had lots of tin which is an important ingredient of bronze, so the people who lived in Cornwall probably realised they were on to a good thing.

It may be that the Celts introduced Bronze. We know that they came to Britain because they have left us the Welsh, Irish, Scottish and Cornish languages, as well as quite a lot of people with red hair and freckles. I expect they got a mixed reception. Some may have been met by unfriendly residents. It would have been a bit sad for them to have rowed all that way only to be met by a barrage of stones, stone arrows and insults.

Others may have been met by curiosity, and others by no one at all, because there were not many people about then in any case.

Eventually, however, I suppose an early European Free Trade Area came into being, and Bronze took over. One other thing the Celts brought with them was pretty Bronze jewellery, so I expect that women had quite an influence in overcoming resistance.

I'll not have a daughter of mine wearing one of those new fangled danglers! Stone is good enough for your mother, and her mother before her – so it's good enough for you!

Then came the Iron Age. Again, we don't know if there was much resistance from the inhabitants, or whether the needs of trade were paramount even then. Iron was not so nice

47

for making jewellery as bronze, but much better for ploughs and weapons, so in the end it took over. I think it is true to say that the technology for making iron came from abroad in the first place probably with the Celts again; so we can thank men in boats for bringing it to these shores, where our forefathers learned to do great things with it.

After the Celts came the Romans. They gave us nice straight roads, probably with fewer potholes than we have now; underfloor heating, baths; law and order (of a kind, and only for a few hundred years) and Latin.

Then came the Saxons, in their boats, probably needing quite a lot of rowing as well. They gave us Old English, which presumably grew into Modern English, (in addition to whatever came before). From Old English, we certainly gained a lot of very colourful swear words, still in regular use today. There is no need for me to list these, as they are more appropriate to rowing than to rowing.

The Saxons and allied Angles and Jutes also, it seems, gave the people an infusion of fair hair and blue eyes, to add to the Celtic red hair and freckles, and the Roman noses already here. We know that Angles, at least, had fair hair and blue eyes from the story told about Pope Gregory the Great (540 to 604 A.D.), who saw some fair-haired blue-eyed boys up for sale in a Rome slave market. When he asked who they were he was told they were Angles. He is reported to have said "not Angles but Angels." In spite of my enquiring mind getting busy, I am not going to get involved in debating the attitudes of the early Church on Slavery, or why St Gregory seemed to indicate that he believed that Angels had fair hair and blue eyes.

No sooner had the Saxons, Angles and Jutes settled in, than another lot came sailing and rowing to these shores. The Vikings. They gained a fearsome reputation for rape, pillage, and loot, but after a while they settled down and obviously got mixed with the natives to help make us what we are today. The Viking boats were clearly very equipped with oars as well as sails, and they travelled vast distances.

Thinking of the Vikings settling down, reminds me that we older folks will certainly know about King Canute. He was a Viking who became king of England from 1016 until 1035 AD, and has been given a reputation as a good King. Apparently he was a Christian but, as we all know, that does not necessarily make him good. My source of information about this is as follows:

Canute Rebukes His Courtiers by Alphonse-Marie-Adolphe de Neuville

The story of King Canute and the tide is an apocryphal anecdote illustrating the piety or humility of King Canute the Great, recorded in the 12th century by Henry of Huntingdon.

In the story, Canute demonstrates to his flattering courtiers that he has no control over the elements (the incoming tide), explaining that secular power is vain compared to the supreme power of God where the futility of "trying to stop the tide" of an inexorable event is pointed out, but usually misrepresenting Canute as believing he had supernatural powers, when Huntingdon's story in fact relates the opposite.

In Huntingdon's account, Canute set his throne by the seashore and commanded the incoming tide to halt and not wet his feet and robes. Yet continuing to rise as usual (the tide) dashed over his feet and legs without respect to his royal person. Then the king leapt backward, saying "Let all men know how empty and worthless is the power of kings, for there is none worthy of the name but He whom heaven, earth, and sea obey by eternal laws." He then hung his gold crown on a crucifix and never wore it again "to the honour of God the almighty King."

This story has nothing directly to do with the story of rowing, but is the result of my EM asking "what if" questions, i.e. What if King Canute had had a clever and cunning adviser (just like our leaders and everyone else's leaders have these days) to suggest the following action: as it was clear that the King could not stop the tide coming in, a word in the King's ear could have led to this;

- - - THIS MIGHT HAVE HAPPENED - - - .

CUNNING
ADVISER

The Adviser would advise the King to simply turn his throne around to face the shore, and command the tide to come in, as shown below.

As people were probably as gullible then as they can be nowadays, it is likely that the story would have had a much more dramatic influence on history, as well as doing the reputation and income of the cunning adviser a lot of good. One can imagine that he would have staked a lot on convincing the Courtiers that King Canute had divine powers. This could even have led to the creation of a new sect, maybe called "Canutists".

This, in the course of time, would undoubtedly have split, one group called "Canuists", a name even more likely to be given nowadays as the letter "t" seems to be on its way out in pronunciation among young people. The name "Canuists" would tie in nicely with the theme of this book. The other sect would be calling themselves "Nutists". If these sects had survived to this day, this would undoubtedly have caused problems with the very genuine groups who believe in the health benefits of nudity, particularly if the word "nutist" is spoken by someone with a stuffy nose. The spoken version of "nudist" would, if the "t" were pronounced, probably upset those who do valuable conservation work studying newts.

Fortunately, there was no cunning adviser to lead King Canute astray, or if there was, the King rejected his suggestion. Then the next lot of invaders to use oars to get to this country were the Normans. As we know, a whole army of them came across the channel in 1066 and conquered England. There is a famous guide to the conquest in the Bayeux Tapestry. My guidebook to this, bought on a visit several years ago, states, "The Normans' ships were propelled using sails or oars, which meant they could make headway even if there was no wind. The Tapestry mostly shows warships with twenty lines of rowers."

The Normans were, as we know, really Vikings who had taken a liking to Normandy, settled there, and took the trouble to learn French, but that does not have much bearing on this story, other than to mention that rowing was probably in their genes.

So what did the Normans bring to Britain? They brought castles, or at least the skill and the will to build them, much bigger and better than the Saxon ones. The same with cathedrals and churches. They organised everything through the Domesday Book and added French to the language and introduced the feudal system. Perhaps above all they became the English Upper Class, which at once became the Ruling class. This is not to suggest that there would not have been an English Upper Class had Harold won the Battle of Hastings, but he didn't so we will never know. William the Conqueror rewarded his loyal Knights with great chunks of land, some still owned by their antecedents. I find it slightly strange that the ruling class down the centuries has been the most devoted defenders of England, very often in the past against the French, yet they are mostly descended from the French.

The English Upper class created the public schools and the universities. Private schools and grammar schools emulated them, and most of those had rowing clubs. Where would rowing in this country be today had it not been for those generations of young men, and in more recent times, women, who rowed so magnificently for school, club, or university and country?

At this point, I want to make it clear that I am in no way prejudiced against the Upper Class. They have, down the years, produced some great leaders, explorers, academics, scientists, etc., the list is endless. It is quite possible that the sport of rowing helped give them the qualities that made them great. Up until the last century, the Upper Class was indeed the ruling class, but times have changed. The Ruling classes today are more likely to be drawn from the worlds of banking, industry, or professional politicians. This is the same in all countries. All have their class structures, and the governing "elites". Whenever a Ruling Class is overthrown or replaced, it is inevitably replaced in turn by the victors of the change who become the new Ruling Class. These comments are merely my Enquiring Mind getting busy, and have nothing to do with the story of rowing.

However, my EM will not let me leave the subject of the Normans without trying to answer some questions raised by my looking at this extract from the Bayeux Tapestry.

Bayeux Tapestry

3 things in particular puzzled me:

1. Both sides look the same, all in chain mail, and all wearing the same sort of helmet.
2. These helmets all have nose protectors.
3. The Normans are the only ones on horseback.

Let me share my thoughts on each of these issues in turn. First, the lookalike problem:

Unless opposing armies had some means of distinguishing one from the other, there would have been terrible confusion in battle. Maybe that's how banners and trumpets came into use; otherwise, this situation could have arisen:

I THINK WE'RE ON THE SAME SIDE..

If the warriors only communicated by shouting, any English army fighting foreigners would have been at a great disadvantage because foreigners usually speak English better than English speakers speak foreign languages, so they would understand the English commands.

Secondly, the matter of nose protectors: How did the helmet makers cope with the many different sizes and types of nose that were around (and still are)?

HERE ARE A FEW EXAMPLES

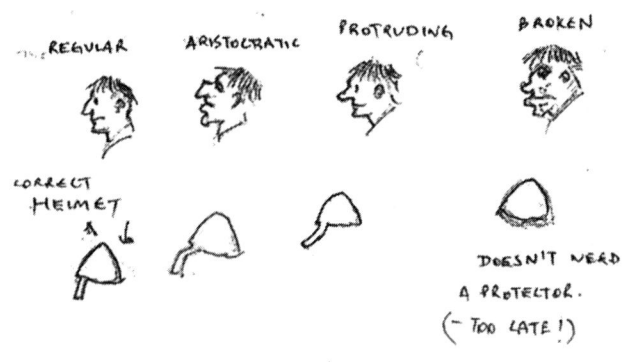

I expect that somewhere there is a book on "Nose Protectors in the Construction of Helmets, 1066–1200" or something like that, but my limited research ability has not found it. There must have been a standard nose protector, maybe called a Standard Nasal Orifice Type (SNOT for short) helmet. Even this, however, would cause problems. We have seen that the upper-class Normans were those on horseback, but even they didn't come in a standard size—some would have smaller heads than others, and the SNOT helmet would be too big for some, so that the wearer would have to hold his head back in order to see.

This may have led to the expression "looking down his nose". This leads logically to dealing with the third thing that puzzled me about the picture from the Bayeux Tapestry, i.e. that the Normans were the only ones on horses. This can be explained by assuming that the mounted warriors were only those who could afford horses or be provided with them by their lords and masters. It is a fact, even to this day, that having a horse must be quite an expensive thing. You either have to have a lot of money or be willing to be poor in order to have your horse. In olden times such as we think of when talking about the Normans, and throughout the Middle Ages, it would certainly only be the lords and knights who could afford horses or provide them for their minions. As mentioned earlier, as even the mounted soldiers all looked alike in the Tapestry, you can't tell who was a lord, a knight, or a mounted minion.

I find it interesting that, from what I have read, the mounted warrior and later the cavalry have always been regarded as the elite of soldiers. There is a certain logical inevitability that those on their high horses simply have to look down on those on foot. As the lords and knights must have spent a lot of time on horseback both in battle and when hunting, this could well have become an attitude of mind, inbred into those of the elite and therefore ruling classes of the day. Some would still have the attitude even when not on their horses. Add this to my other theory about the effect of the nose protectors on helmets, and you could have another explanation for class attitudes.

Fortunately, these have changed a lot over the years, both from the point of view of those who felt they were superior and those who didn't like being looked down on.

I apologise for writing so much about our class system, but as the Normans played such a big part in bringing it to Britain, it must, I feel, be mentioned when thinking about the impact of their conquest, and the major part played in this by the humble oar, and the no doubt humble oarsmen.

I want to make one final observation before moving on, namely that I find it funny that you can "look down" on someone even if they are taller than you.

After the Normans, there were no more invasions. Rowing would go on mostly as a necessary way of getting to and from ships, crossing rivers and lakes, fishing, etc. Punting may have been more of a leisure activity in this country, so perhaps canoeing was too. This is something I don't know. There were a few outstanding rowers, however, who come to mind from the years before it became a sport. It is worth mentioning

Captain Bligh of the ship H.M.S. Bounty, who, in 1789, was cast adrift in an open boat in the Pacific Ocean by mutineers, with some fellow officers and loyal sailors. They managed to row for several weeks, eventually reaching Timor. Of course, we don't know if he did much actual rowing himself, maybe just shouting instructions to his crew, such as "left hand down a bit!" It is, however, generally assumed that he navigated.

Another famous rower was Grace Darling when, in 1838, she became a national heroine. She and her father, a lighthouse keeper, rowed through a storm to rescue the survivors of a shipwreck on the Farne Islands. Another famous feat of rowing worth mentioning was that undertaken by Sir Ernest Shackleton in 1916. His ship got crushed in the ice in Antarctica, and he and 5 of his crew rowed 800 miles in an open boat to get help. There may well have been others, but for the purposes of this "Story of Rowing", I want to look at the impact of rowing on other parts of the world, and come back to looking at the present day and the future of rowing, canoeing, and punting in this country later on.

Chapter 6
The Impact of Rowing on the Middle Eastern Countries

This can only be described as being responsible for the early development of the whole vast region, and indeed of the whole ancient world. At a time when we Brits were struggling to get the roof on Stonehenge, the Ancient Greeks were trading and making war in galleys, big wooden boats powered by sail and innumerable rowers. The Romans, too, had galleys, and may even have used them to carry their armies over to Britain. In fact, galleys of several different designs were used throughout history; after Greeks, Phoenicians, Romans, Byzantines, Ottomans, Venetians, North African Corsairs, even, I was surprised to read, Russians. At the time of Peter The Great, they were used both in the calmer waters of the Baltic during his wars against the Swedes, and all the way down to the Black Sea to fight the Turks. My book told me he found it more efficient to build a Galley-making shipyard near the Turkish border than to make them nearer home and have to get them rowed all the way down.

We can't, of course, ignore the Vikings when thinking about the impact of the humble Oar on the history of this region. They even rowed down through what today is Russia, maybe mostly as traders, down those big rivers that come into the Baltic from a long way inland, but also into the Black Sea. Later, they conquered much of Italy, Sicily, and many other places. It is, however, the Galley that has done the most in the history of the Mediterranean. It is the story of the Galley that has caused my own Enquiring Mind to get going yet again, on what may seem to be at the very least a tangent from the main theme. I had to investigate further.

My trusty Oxford English Reference Dictionary describes the Galley as follows:

'The galley was the oared fighting ship of the Mediterranean, dating from about 3000 BC and lasting into the 18th century. Such ships had up to 3 banks of oars (as in the trireme) as well as one or more sails, which were lowered before action. The weapon was the ram, a pointed spur fixed to the bow of the galley on or above the waterline; the Ancient Greek technique of fighting was to ram and then depart at speed, while the Romans preferred to grapple and fight on deck, or use catapult weapons. (My aside… See Charlton Heston in the film Ben Hur to get an idea what it must have been like). To resume from the O.E Ref. dictionary:'

'Slaves and criminals were later sometimes used as rowers' (my comment… As in Ben Hur, although he was, of course, wrongly convicted).

"Although free men were preferred as being more reliable in battle. With its slim light draught design, the galley was an unstable vessel suitable only for calm waters."

I can't help wondering if we are not seeing history repeat itself. In March 2022, the P & O ferry company sacked 800 crew members and replaced them with much cheaper contract workers. Later, a report said that the company was cutting the wages of even those workers. If this goes on, and with fuel prices rocketing as well, at least in 2022, the company will end up using either professionals, slaves, or criminals. As few of these will have had any training in working on ships we could finish up with this scenario:

This would certainly take rowing to an entirely higher level (several levels in fact). But to come back to the galley. What an amazing type of boat! I cannot get my head around how they were designed because they were not only big versions of the more basic rowing (sail-assisted) boats, but galleys also came in different sizes. There were Triremes, with three banks of oars, and Quinqueremes with five banks of oars. My Enquiring Mind got very busy on this subject.

The O.E. Ref. Dictionary as above refers to galleys such as Triremes, having 3 "banks" of oars. I looked up meanings for "banks," and one of these is "a tier of oars". I then looked up the word "tiers," and it says "A row or rank or unit of structure, as one of several placed one above another (tiers of seats)".

This surely must mean that in a trireme there were 3 ranks of rowers, one above the other, and even more remarkable, in a quinquereme there were 5!

I did manage to use my computer to try to resolve this, and one bit of information did confirm that in a trireme there were in fact 3 tiers of rowers, on the bottom tier, one rower per oar, on the middle tier 2 rowers per oar, and on the top tier 3 per oar. Look at the problems this arrangement must have presented to the early trireme boat designers:

This is a cross-section of a trireme, to illustrate the difficulty.

I can think of 3 possible solutions: [1] To have the seats parallel to the lower rank, but to choose different height rowers, the shortest holding the oar nearest to the porthole, the next tallest sitting by him, and so on, etc.

This idea would obviously create severe problems of supply and demand for slaves, criminals, or professionals of the right heights. The second possibility would be the sloping bench. This could, however, lead to the oarsmen furthest away from the porthole slowly sliding down the bench, thus causing a pile-up of rowers near the exit, with a real risk of them all losing their grips on the oar completely.

The third and perhaps the most likely answer to the problem would be to have the rowers sitting on boxes of different heights.

The complexity of design for galleys did not end with seating arrangements. It is obvious that the more ranks of rowers above one another that you have, the longer the oars as we have just outlined, and the wider the galley. This had to be the case to have room for all the oarsmen, and for the longer oars to be pulled on board when the galley came into port.

Finally, how did they make the enormously long oars needed? Perhaps in the earliest galleys, they chose very long tree trunks, but this would have become unsustainable, unless that is why so much of North Africa is now desert. I have read that long ago, even in Roman times, it was a fertile area, which means lots of trees.

One of my favourite cartoonists is Edward Heath Robinson. I am sure he would have been able to come up with a solution to the extra-long oar problem.

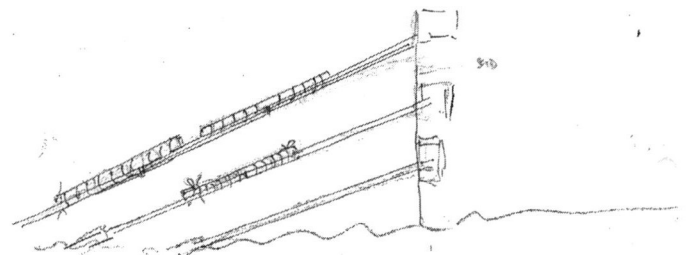

Chapter 7
The Impact of Rowing on the Americas, North, South, East, West & Middle

When I first considered this, I didn't think there could be much to say. I've read that the earliest humans probably walked there, over that narrow bit that now separates Alaska from Russia, but which may once have been joined to the continent we now call America. If they couldn't walk on dry land, then maybe they walked over when it was frozen. At the time of my writing this, relations between Russia and America, and indeed between Russia and the rest of the world are strained, to put it mildly, and a spokesman for Russia was quoted as suggesting that they, the Russians, could have a claim on Alaska, because Russian people settled there many years ago. It doesn't help to think of the consequences of any attempt by Russians to repeat the crossing made by their far-off ancestors, who weren't members of any nation, in any case. Those were the days when people were either Neanderthals or Homo sapiens, and as we have seen already, it is reckoned they must have got on quite well with one another for a few thousand years. One thing is certain of course, is that any movement of people from Russia to America nowadays would not be by rowing boat, as the Bering Straits are wide and rough. This scenario does not, therefore, come into the Story of Rowing.

Returning to that theme, then, it dawned on me that the impact of rowing on the history of the Americas was immense, and life-changing for the Native peoples. How else, other than by rowing, could the Conquistadors, the Pilgrim Fathers, and all the other European invaders and settlers have got ashore from their sailing ships without rowing boats? There were no ready-made harbours when the first Europeans arrived.

We know, of course, that they didn't really forget their oars, but it is a good exercise for the Enquiring Mind to think of the possible result if they had done so. It might even have had some effect on the history of their home countries if boatloads of disgruntled sailors and hopeful settlers had to sail back over those stormy oceans on a diet of weevil-ridden biscuits, salt pork, and seagulls after setting eyes on the lands they hoped would give them untold wealth and/or freedom, because they couldn't get ashore. The rowing boat has much to answer for in the minds of those Native Americans who may feel bitter about the coming of so many foreigners, and what happened to their cultures as a result.

It is worth noting that the Story of Mankind's moving on water by manual methods has been greatly influenced by means employed by Native Americans.

The Inuit gave us the Kayak, and the Anorak to wear to keep the paddler warm.

The tribes of the Eastern and Southern States of the USA were experts in canoeing. The design of their birch bark canoes has been copied in fibreglass and plastic, and can be seen on lakes and rivers throughout the world. Both kayaking and canoeing are Olympic sports.

Once the Europeans came to the northern parts, Canada and USA, whether as traders or invaders, they, too, took to canoeing as the best way to get around the area's mighty rivers. They must surely have picked up the skills from the Native Americans. Relations between traders and the Native Americans can't have been too bad in the early days. Both the English and the French had Indian tribes fighting for them, and the fur traders who explored much of Canada probably depended on them to find their way. The majority of those traders/explorers were French, who canoed their way into uncharted territory in search of beaver and other animal pelts for what was a very lucrative trade for the benefit of the wealthy ladies of Europe.

They often had to carry their large canoes overland to get around formidable rapids. That would have been very hard and potentially dangerous work, and maybe that is where the value of having one member of the team to guide the rest, i.e. a Cox, was realised.

Great concentration would be essential for the man (not much, if any, mention of women in this time of exploration) responsible for guiding the team if disasters were to be avoided.

The French Voyageurs, as they were called, were employed to carry the goods to the trading posts, normally run by the Hudson Bay Company, where the mostly English shopkeepers (as Napoleon said, the English are a nation of shopkeepers) did the business bit.

As for the USA, the settled Europeans eventually took up rowing as a sport in a big way. In fact, I have heard it said that it is the oldest sport in the USA. They must have been very good at it, because it is a fact that both Oxford and Cambridge Universities would offer big, strong American university students notional courses of study at our universities so that they could qualify to row in the Boat Race teams. This was in my lifetime. Maybe the practice has stopped now, as it would eventually be self-defeating when both Oxford and Cambridge crews had equal numbers of big strong Americans, so they might as well revert to homegrown rowers. I never heard an explanation as to why the Americans at that time were apparently so much bigger and stronger than our own rowers. Maybe it was a leftover from the wartime rationing that produced weedier men for a while in this country. If any of the Oxbridge teams came from state schools, they could blame school dinners, but even the public school lads would have probably grown up on the physically toughening regimes of their schools, cold showers, and thin gruel. In any case, importing big, strong American rowers would have created some problems.

If the big strong American is placed in the front of this boat, the cox has to lean out in order to see past him because he is so much wider than the rest of the crew.

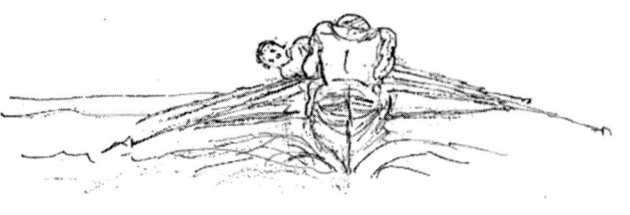

EFFECT OF PLACING VERY BIG AMERICAN IN THE
CENTRE OF THE BOAT

Chapter 8
Rowing & Africa & Asia.

As there is plenty of evidence that all humans originally came from Africa, it is logical to assume that all the means of crossing water were discovered on that continent. The Ancient Egyptians certainly knew about rowing, as I mentioned earlier in this narrative. Maybe the oar itself was an African invention. There are no doubt people today on Africa's rivers and lakes going about their daily work by rowing or paddling or punting, although the invention of the outboard motor will have replaced the oar and paddle as the means of propulsion in many instances. In a number of parts of Africa, of course, getting around in small craft of any kind must have its dangers due to irritable hippopotamuses and hungry crocodiles.

Of course, the arrival of Europeans, as with the Americas, rowing ashore from their sailing ships had the most enormous impact on the Africans. I can't say more about rowing and Africa, so we'll move on.

Rowing & Asia

I haven't been able to find much information about rowing specifically in this vast area. Arabs had dhows, and the Chinese had junks, but both of these were sailing boats. I have seen with my own eyes fishing boats off the coast of Sri Lanka, mostly sailboats, which were able to come ashore onto the beach, although there is no reason to suppose they didn't also have oars. These were probably the same sort of boats one would see off the coast of India. However, I have learned of a most unusual type of rowing used on certain rivers in Vietnam. This came from a TV programme in which Sue Perkins was doing a trip along the Mekong River. She came upon a group of people who were actually rowing with their feet! Here are two photos to prove it.

I remembered this when wondering what, if anything, I could write about rowing in Asia and have found out a little bit more about this very unusual way of doing it. My computer told me that this was developed by villagers in a particularly beautiful stretch of the Mekong River on which they acted as guides, taking tourists in the locals' sampans. You can imagine how difficult it would be to row the conventional way while watching where you were going at the same time as giving a running commentary.

However, this has awakened my EM and imagination, and I have a theory that there may be another factor that led to the development of foot rowing. It could be because of the hats worn by the Vietnamese. They have undoubtedly been developed over thousands of years and are eminently suitable for keeping the rain off and the sun, but not so practical for traditional rowing. Unless the hat is a very good, tight fit, when the wearer tries to turn their head, all they see is the inside of the hat. I have had exactly the same problem when walking in the mountains in bad weather, with the hood of my anorak zipped up well against the elements. Trying to turn your head a bit to look back or sideways, and all you see is the inside of the hood. You have to do a nearly complete body turn in order to see behind, which in mountains takes your vision away from where you are going and could lead to your falling off the edge. On a busy river, having to turn round completely every now and again could lead to collisions. For that reason alone, rowing with one's feet while facing the direction of travel must be a great advantage, and you could keep your traditional hat.

Unfortunately, my EM has got into action on an aspect of this subject that has nothing to do with rowing, namely, how did the Knights of old manage? By the latter part of the Middle Ages, I have read that they were often very heavily armoured, well bolted into their helmets as well. They must have had the same problem if they wanted to turn around at all. This must have meant having to turn your whole horse round as well to see what was going on behind. Could this partly explain how the English army won the Battle of Agincourt against the might of French Chivalry?

My Oxford English Reference Dictionary says that this victory was largely thanks to the successful use of the longbow by the English, and I have always been a bit puzzled how an arrow could pierce heavy armour. I wonder if the following may have happened!

The French nobility on their great chargers, both horse and rider protected by heavy armour which the arrows were simply bouncing off, advancing steadily towards the English, getting into position to charge, a seemingly invincible wall of steel. They are led by either the French King or one of his great nobles, riding heroically in front of his Knights. An arrow hits the shield of a nearby rider and ricochets against his back. He feels the impact but thinks it is one of his men trying to get his attention, bearing in mind he cannot hear a shout because of his massively thick and well screwed-on helmet. As we have pointed out, he cannot turn his head to check for the same reason, so he has to turn his horse around completely to see if someone wants to attract his attention. His disciplined and devoted followers take this to be a signal for them to do the same, so they all turn completely round. This exposes the only unprotected part of their Great Warhorses, namely their bottoms, to the English arrows which find an easy target. Obviously, the horses don't take kindly to this, career off through the ranks of the French army, causing complete chaos, and handing the victory to the English. I am fully aware that even if this explanation for the English victory could be proven to be true, it would never be accepted to be taught in our schools, because we are far too proud of the better-known version of the Battle. No history student should therefore quote my suggested alternative.

The thought about the Battle of Agincourt and the clash of armoured knights against archers has, however, led me to consider wider historical implications. When I was younger, history was much more inclined to focus on great English victories rather than the broader context. One such victory was against the French at the Battle of Crecy in 1346. This victory, too, was more attributable to English archers than to heavy knights. The regrettable aspect of this is that it indicates the French ruling elite learned nothing between Crecy in 1346 and Agincourt in 1415. However, our military commanders have not been very different. They sent soldiers in red coats with muskets against the American revolutionaries armed with rifles, ultimately losing that colony. They sent soldiers in red coats against the Boers in the First Boer War, costing hundreds of lives. They dispatched thousands of cavalrymen to the Western Front in WW1, thinking they could charge to victory, and initially sent our armies ill-prepared to face either the Nazis or the Japanese in WW2.

I have a cynical thought that this mindset stemmed from the belief that simply being British was sufficient to guarantee victory, a legacy of those proud Normans mentioned earlier. I hope this attitude is a thing of the past, although some opinions expressed during the Brexit campaign about foreigners give cause to wonder if things have changed that much.

These are, of course, my own views and have nothing to do with the story of rowing directly. However, they illustrate how one's Enquiring Mind can lead to different topics. This brief historical review of military errors contrasts with the world of rowing, which has undoubtedly evolved with the times. I'm unsure if women faced challenges in being recognised as rowers, but they are certainly prominent nowadays.

Returning to the topic of foot rowing, it's surprising that it hasn't been more widely adopted. In leisure boating, such as punting, where gallant young men guide elegant young ladies down tranquil rivers, foot rowing could liberate the punter to sit with his companion in comfort, reading poetry, singing love songs, or using his smartphone, while his feet handle the rowing.

This could eventually spell the end of punting, leaving it as the preserve of a few enthusiasts. If foot rowing were ever considered beyond the Mekong River, it would provide both opportunities and difficulties, just like any new idea. The pictures of the Vietnamese foot rowers don't show how, if at all, the oars are attached to the feet. I could guess that if they were attached, it would be by cloth bandages. A more sophisticated method could be devised. I give below my suggestions:

1. Shows a fitting for a foot operating one oar. The fitting 'shoe' would obviously be the other way round for the other foot.

   1a shows what it would look like on a foot.

2. Shows a "shoe" to fit both feet if two feet could be used to row.

   2a shows an extension fitting if two feet could be used simultaneously.

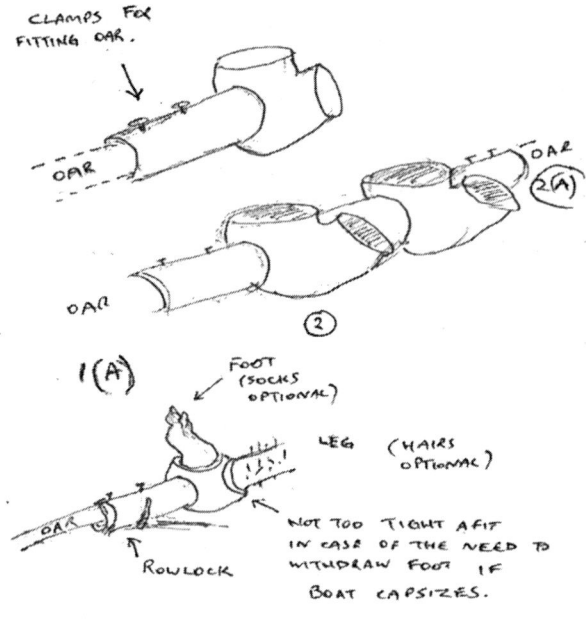

CLAMPS FOR FITTING OAR.

OAR

OAR

OAR (2A)

OAR (2)

1(A)

FOOT (SOCKS OPTIONAL)

LEG (HAIRS OPTIONAL)

OAR

ROWLOCK

NOT TOO TIGHT A FIT IN CASE OF THE NEED TO WITHDRAW FOOT IF BOAT CAPSIZES.

FOR SIMPLY MESSING ABOUT ON THE RIVER, FOOT ROWING WOULD HAVE SEVERAL ADVANTAGES :—

afterthought :— This is more likely to be
a Kindle or a smart phone than an actual
book .. —

When it came to racing, there would need to be further changes. For example, the need for a cox could be eliminated because the crew would be facing the direction of travel, and in any case, the crew would require different seating, so boats would need the extra space to accommodate it. I have no idea how foot rowing would compete with traditional rowing in respect of speed, but a Boat Race between Oxford and Cambridge would make entertaining viewing. It would not be long before someone came up with the idea of both foot and arm operation of oars. What amazing speed could then be achieved!

Of course, Foot Rowing requires a different technique to rowing in the traditional way. Because, provided you are sitting facing the direction of travel as the Vietnamese in the pictures are clearly doing, the rower needs to push with his/her feet. Normal rowing requires the rower to pull on the oar. If you are gently drifting along, the arms can do all the work, but if you want to travel at speed, the legs are needed as well to get maximum pull. It is a fact that leg muscles are stronger than arms, but controlling the oars by foot requires a lot of practice. This would, however, need great coordination skills, which women might be better at than men. My wife tells me that women can more easily think of more than one thing at a time than men can, and I am sure she is right, certainly as far as I am concerned. Using feet and arms on separate oars would also need greater effort and stamina. I'm sure someone would have a go, though. Leaving readers with those thoughts, I will move on with this around the worldview of the impact of rowing.

Chapter 9
Rowing & The Pacific

Apart from the now familiar scenario of rowing being the way explorers, traders, and missionaries got ashore on Pacific islands, or on Australia and New Zealand (with the same results on original inhabitants as in the Americas), it is rafting and canoeing that most Pacific peoples used to travel the ocean. Explorers found that Polynesian-type people were found on the most remote islands, and there was much head scratching among anthropologists as to how this happened. A Norwegian anthropologist named Thor Heyerdahl proved a theory that the Polynesians could have come on rafts from Peru to the Pacific Islands. He and his team built a raft out of balsa logs, and allowed it to mainly drift on the currents across the sea to make landfall near Tahiti. I seem to recall reading that the balsa wood got rather worryingly soggy by the end of the journey, but they survived. This was in 1947. To think I was 7 years old at the time!

I have read that Pacific Islanders also used big war canoes and catamarans to get around and were brilliant navigators.

How the New Zealanders became so good at Rugby?
(This is just a legend created by my EM)

The story begins in England at the early stages of the Industrial Revolution, before the railways were developed, and the transport of materials and goods was dependent on canals. During those years, at the end of the 18th Century perhaps, one Jemmy Leggett was born. We don't know exactly when or where, but it must have been near canals, because he grew up to find work on the canal boats, plying their trade between ports and factories. In those days, canal boats were pulled by horses plodding along the towpaths. However, when a canal had to go through a tunnel, the horse had to be untied from the boat and led over the hill through which the tunnel had been dug, to collect the boat when it emerged on the other side. This was because tunnels were seldom, if ever, wide or high enough for the horse to continue through. The method of pushing a canal boat through the tunnel without horsepower was for the crew to lie on their backs and use their legs to push on the roof or sides of the tunnel, thus propelling the boat along. This was called "legging it", and might even have been the origin of our hero's name. After all, people who baked gave the name Baker, people who smithed gave their name to Smith, so why not people who legged it becoming Leggett's? That, however, is not important to our story. This way of pushing a canal boat through narrow tunnels must have been very hard work, but one benefit would be the development of very strong leg muscles, a factor to be kept in mind as my story continues.

[Cut out cross-section of canal tunnel showing crew legging it.]

← DIRECTION OF TRAVEL

Young Jemmy was doing quite well on the boats, hard though it was, until one day he had the misfortune to encounter a Press gang. In those days, the Royal Navy was finding it difficult to recruit sailors, so they used to send gangs around the country to trick healthy young men into "taking the King's shilling", which once inadvertently done, committed the taker to a life on the ocean wave. This was often done in pubs, by getting the victim drunk, and slipping him a coin. I don't know if press-ganged sailors were given any sort of contract, but if they were, you can be sure it would be for a very long period of service.

Anyway, this is what happened to poor Jemmy. It was a tough life aboard HMs ships of war, and the lad would have been lucky to survive long on a diet of salt pork, weevil-ridden biscuits, and seagulls, to say nothing of storms, battles, beatings, and scurvy. In fact, though, it was a storm that led Jemmy to his salvation and to the gift of rugby to New Zealand. This is because, somewhere off the coast of those islands, his ship was wrecked in a storm. Somehow Jem was able to cling on to a bit of wreckage, and eventually was washed up on a beach in the territory of a great Māori chief.

Now, as I am sure everyone knows, the Māoris were a very fierce and warlike people. They still are if the performance of their war dance prior to rugby matches is anything to go by.

Lurking in the dim recesses of my memory are two things I have read about the Māoris, which may or may not be true:

1. That they were cannibals.
2. That they used to launch their war canoes over the bodies of captives taken in battle or raids on other tribes.

The first is a very upsetting suggestion to the present-day Māoris, being as they no doubt are, law-abiding New Zealanders. The second is also a bit upsetting, though every nation and tribe down the centuries has been guilty of even worse things. The other point against this method of launching canoes is that it would have been terribly inefficient. It is very unlikely that the same captive could have been used more than once, and also captives of the same thickness would have been needed to create a level launching pad.

For the sake of this narrative, however, both or either of these may have been in the minds of Jemmy's captors, because for some reason they kept him alive, and for whatever purpose they decided to fatten him up. In the condition he was in when he was found on the beach, he was no use for anything; whether for eating, as a canoe launcher, or even as a canoe pusher if perhaps logs were used as rollers for launching purposes (a logical alternative method to method 2 above, which may just be a nasty rumour spread by people who didn't like Māoris). Jemmy was therefore preserved for whatever reason, and a long time passed without him getting any fatter. He clearly managed to learn a bit of Māori language, and could listen in to the discussions going on in the tribe, and he soon cottoned on to the big problem facing the great Chief. It was this; the more successful his tribe was in wars and raids against other tribes and on other islands, the further his warriors had to go to get more captives. The further they had to travel, the bigger the canoes that were needed, the bigger the canoe, the more captives needed to launch them, by whatever method and so on. The intelligent Chief could see real problems ahead.

Now, in spite of his humble background, Jem was also an intelligent chap, and he suddenly thought of a way out for the tribe, which would be an efficient use of resources both human and material. He sought an audience with the chief, and recalling his past life as a canal boat legger in far-off England, he came up with the following plan:

1. The canoe launch team would lie in a row on the beach, on their backs almost in the surf, with their legs in the air.

2. The canoe would then be lifted onto the row of feet.

3. On the command "run", they would all execute that with the leg movements. The beach stays where it is, but the canoe is pushed fast into the sea.

This was exactly the leg movement used to push canal boats through tunnels, and the Chief immediately understood the thinking behind Jemmy's suggestion. It worked so well that it became a "game changer" for the tribe. They achieved quicker launchings without needing as many captives. The logical result of that, of course, was that they no longer needed to make as many raids, therefore fewer launchings, and the launch teams could be used over and over again. After a while, the local lads of the tribe reckoned they could do it themselves without the need for any captives at all, at least for launching purposes. Friendly contests developed between tribes; indeed, canoe launching became almost a sport. The Māoris gradually developed the massive legs and thighs that such an activity produced, as well as the ability to move those legs and thighs quickly.

However, that was by no means the end of the story. With fewer canoe launchings needed, the tribes' young men had more time on their hands, which they spent messing about on the beaches, idly kicking the odd coconut that washed ashore on the ocean currents (a painful pastime in bare feet). Then one day, a round, somewhat softer thing was washed up. Jemmy, who had been made an Honorary Māori in recognition of his brilliant idea, and was now just one of the lads, recognized it as a football. This must have been swept overboard from a consignment of footballs destined for the convicts in Australia. Although salt-hardened and barnacle-encrusted, this was much less painful to kick around than a coconut. However, even that caused toes to be bruised, until one day, one of the Māoris accidentally sat on the ball, squashing it into the now-familiar shape of the rugby ball we know so well.

The group soon found what fun they could have with the revised-shaped ball, by picking it up and throwing it to each other. Hence, the noble game of Rugby took root in New Zealand. Later on, no doubt, a colonial administrator came along to teach them the rules, and we all know the rest of the story.

The massive thighs and legs became genetically part of the structure of the New Zealander, as well as the ability to get the maximum speed out of them. Jemmy, by the way, married a local girl and lived happily ever after.

Chapter 10
Rowing as It Is Today

I hope that I have been able to convince anyone reading this of the supreme importance of rowing in the development of the human race. None of us would be where we are today if someone in the very distant past, somewhere in the world, hadn't discovered rowing, canoeing, and rafting as ways to get across water. Like every technical invention made by people, rowing, etc. has been used by people for both good and bad purposes, but the main reasons for moving about on water have remained the same down the ages. We can safely say that this country at least is unlikely to be invaded by enemies in rowing boats, canoes, or rafts. We will therefore concentrate on the activity in its best uses, sport and leisure.

The more my EM has got to work on this comparatively simple activity, the more things come into my mind on the impact it has had on so many aspects of our lives. We know, for example, that it is good for our health, both physical and mental. It is very good for the environment. It is an excellent competitive sport for both men and women, and it is good for the UK as our professional rowers and canoeists seem very good at it.

There are also several expressions that have come into our language that can or do relate to rowing and the related activities:

"Paddle your own canoe." This isn't a very nice thing to say to anyone, as it means "it's time you coped on your own and stop coming back to me for help."

"Putting your oar in." Not very nice either, as it means "shut up and stop interfering."

"Up the creek without a paddle." You are in a very difficult situation with no obvious way out.

There may be more, and with a stretch of the imagination, we could include "Pride comes before a fall" if the following scenario should ever occur.

And I wonder if regular rowers ever use the word "Rowlocks" when something goes wrong, instead of the more usual "bollocks"?

Another expression that may be derived from rowing is 'We must all pull together.' This could, of course, come from the sport of Tug of War.

We are often told to "All pull together" in order to succeed in what we as a nation or a business want to achieve, or at least what our leaders want to achieve. If they are thinking in the rowing sense, if we all pull together, we will go forward quickly and smoothly. If they are thinking in the Tug of War context, we may still win, but it can mean the winning team falling backwards at high speed, and ending up on the ground with muddy bums, just like the losers.

Whenever we are exhorted by our leaders to "All pull together," we must hope they are referring to the example of a rowing team, and not of a Tug of War team.

What else can rowing, canoeing or punting show us?

As far as I am aware, fair play is one thing. I cannot imagine how you can cheat. Perhaps rowers or canoeists could take steroids, but competitors are vigorously checked these days. I don't think that taking steroids would be thought necessary by anyone doing punting, unless it was part of a longer-term strategy by a fellow to impress his girlfriend. I suppose the following could just happen:

A lady rower's lament:

It is no disgrace,

To lose a race,

But cheating I detest,

So I wonder who,

In the other crew,

Put a spider down my vest?

These activities must also teach participants to look out for others using the water. It is obvious that more people than ever before are using the waterways. Gone are the days for most people when rowing, canoeing, or punting were done out of necessity. They are mostly leisure or sporting pastimes, and care must be taken of other water users.

Fishermen, for example. This could happen:

Or this:

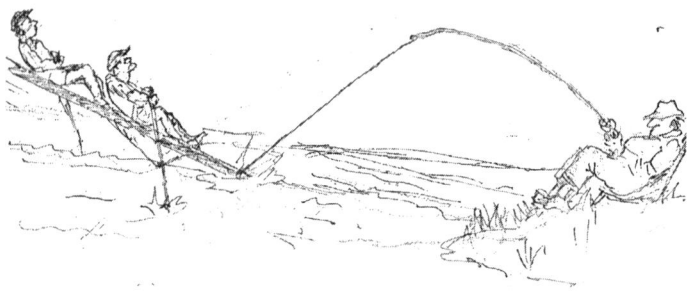

And lookout for other boats:

This latter scenario, of course, should be in the Notes for Guidance to powerboat drivers, as much as for guidance to rowers.

As I hoped I have made clear at the beginning of this book, there is very little I have written about rowing, or its related water crossing methods that is based on personal experience. I have on very rare occasions ventured forth upon the waters in conventional rowing boats, just enough to realise that keeping in a straight line and trying to avoid other boats was not easy for me. However, thinking about this book has reminded me of just two such occasions that are relevant to the theme because they have led my EM up yet another channel, which I will reveal:

The first event took place in the Netherlands, and involved me taking my Dutch father-in-law for a trip in a rowing boat on the Biesbos, a large watery nature reserve near the City of Dordrecht. I cannot remember why, with my lack of skill, I offered to row. It can't have been to help gain his approval to marry his daughter, because we were already married with two children. Maybe I wanted to show that I, from a seafaring nation, had a drop of Nelson's blood in my veins. That expression, "A seafaring Nation" is a bit overdone. For many centuries the majority of British people never saw the sea in their whole lives, unless they were forced to emigrate, press ganged into the Navy, sent to Australia as convicts, or joined the Army to expand or create our Empire.) The Dutch do remind us gently now and again that they beat us quite soundly at sea in the17th Century. I now think I was quite brave to have a go, with a Dutchman as passenger for whom the ability to row is as inbred as the ability to swim. This would be particularly true of a citizen of Dordrecht, which, like so much of the west of the Netherlands, is several metres below sea level. In the great flood of 1953, when dykes broke, and more than1800 people were drowned in the Netherlands, my father-in-law actually rowed to work through the City. Fortunately for Dordrecht the water there came over the dykes, not through them.

However, for whatever reason I took the oars, it was not a success. There came a heavy thunderstorm, and after zigzagging across the bows of several other boats, I managed to steer us up a creek with less water in it than was in the boat.

My second memorable water adventure was in Norway, when with my wife and son, I let myself in for a white water rafting trip along an extremely fast river. Due to a mistake with the starting date for this, we missed the first day, which involved learning how to survive if thrown out of the rubber boat, or if it capsized, which seemed very likely at times. I was a bit apprehensive because I had told a little lie about my ability to swim, which is not great but which was a requirement for taking part. Fortunately I only fell into the boat, not out of it. It was a very exhilarating experience, and I am only relating this because, like the first event, it had me in a rowing boat with sometimes more water in the boat than outside it. These episodes have led me into wondering how professionals cope with having open boats in pouring rain. This could be quite relevant if boats have to be carried any distance from the vehicles that take them to other clubs' rivers for competitions.

If they carry the boats to the water this way, for the benefit of the crews, this could happen:

If they carry them so that they are exposed to the elements, the boats will fill up with water before they even get to the launching place, with this result.

It's indeed true that incidents of boats sinking during the Oxford-Cambridge Boat Race have occurred, although the causes might vary. While weather conditions, including rain, could potentially contribute to such incidents, other factors such as collision with obstacles or technical failures could also be at play. Unfortunately, I don't have a specific answer to this problem either.

Chapter 11
A Grand Festival of Rowing

I hope that I have been able to clearly convey to readers the significant impact that rowing has had on the history of the world, and in particular on this country. At the beginning of this book I was 78 years old. Now, at this juncture, I am 83 years old. Much like my rowing, my progress in writing this book has been slow, and just like my rowing my EM has meandered in various directions. Nevertheless, while it has taken me considerable time to reach this point, rowing, canoeing, punting, and rafting remain vibrant activities. Therefore, I aim for my Story of Rowing to conclude with a hopeful and positive suggestion from my train of thought, rather than merely posing a speculative "What if?" question, more of a "How about trying this idea?" enquiry. So here it is:

Let us hold a Grand Festival of the Oar.

As of the current year, 2024, the world appears to be in a state of disarray, more so than when I started this book in 2018. This country, in particular, seems to be adrift. We have problems in common with many other countries, of course, but it feels as though we have lost our direction as a nation. To my mind, we seem to have rowed ourselves up a creek just like I did once; our boat is taking on water, our confidence in the boat's leadership is shaky, with several previous captains thrown overboard by a discontented crew. We are eagerly awaiting a tide to lift us out once more. At times like these our spirits need uplifting, and what better way than through a Festival.

This is not an entirely novel concept. There was the Great Exhibition of 1851, though its aim was not solely to uplift the nation's spirits, more to try to show the world how wonderful we were. We then had the Festival of Britain in 1951, which did have a strong cheering up element in its purpose. I attended that event, as I had an uncle in Lewisham at the time. I cannot say it necessarily lifted my spirits as the Skylon and the Festival Hall were a bit above the head of an 11-year-old. However, it was quite an enjoyable day out. I expect I had an ice cream if rationing allowed such luxuries.

We have recently witnessed the coronation of King Charles III, but as monarchies are a bit controversial not everyone was cheered up by the event, therefore a different sort of festival might be a good idea.

May I suggest that oars, paddles, and poles are neutral objects and the vast majority of people would agree that it is only the use that they have been put to that could be a matter for discussion. Since rowing and similar activities are predominantly leisure pursuits in most countries and proven to be beneficial for both body and soul, what better cause for celebration?

Let us consider some practical questions arising from this proposal:

1. Where should it be held?

Clearly, the Oar (and its counterparts) does not belong to any single nation, so the celebration of it should be international. However, this presents its own challenges, for the following reasons:

(A) There are a lot of countries where rowing has had little or no impact on their history. Countries with no coastlines and those that are mostly desert come to mind.
(B) Other countries may have more pressing things to think about, such as famine or war, to want to celebrate oars etc.
(C) It would be difficult to decide where such a festival should be held. It would take time and money, and could cause stress between countries, something to be avoided. There is enough of that about as it is.

Therefore I propose that the U.K. should host this festival, for several reasons:

1. Suitable waterways are necessary. Any procession of rowing or paddling boats would be best on river. Most continental rivers are too big and too busy (they actually use their rivers for commercial purposes). This likely applies to the rivers in the U.S.A., African rivers are out of the question, being too large, swift, remote, and inhabited by crocodiles and hippos. I doubt if many African or indeed Asian countries would want to host such an event in any case. However, their participation would be invaluable, indeed essential, for the festival's success. Lakes are

suitable for competitive racing, but if you want to see boats of all shapes and sizes, you need a narrower waterway to enable spectators on the banks to watch. The sea is unsuitable for most rowing events. Therefore, a river like the Thames appears to be the most appropriate choice.

2. The use of my EM in this book, has made me come to the conclusion, that this country has been affected in its history more than most by invaders or settlers coming by rowing (very often sail assisted, of course), thus it seems fitting for the UK to host this festival. While our history has been marked by conflict and tensions between Celts and Romans, Romans and Saxons, Saxons and Vikings, Vikings and Normans, the mixture has shaped our identity. This proposed Festival would serve as an excellent reminder of our collective past. I believe we need such to foster unity.

3. Having lived through two coronations, several state funerals, and countless parades for many reasons, I believe this country excels in pageantry. This Festival could be yet another excuse for a grand display, for all the world to marvel at!

Now let's get down to some ideas for the Grand Festival. Throughout the duration of the celebrations , events could be organised across the country, on rivers, lakes and ponds. Maybe Galleys could re-enact historic battles, and Viking longboats again come up our rivers, to pretend to sack and pillage. Rowing clubs could offer free trips and tuition, (count me out, I'm too old), while canoes and kayaks tackle weirs and waterfalls. Rafts and punts could crowd canals and lakes, and why not bring over some gondolas from Venice?

However, the most spectacular event of the Festival would have to be the Grand Regatta, a great gathering of boats representing the diverse peoples who have used rowing boats throughout history, and those who arrived on these islands by rowing. Boats representing the modern use of oars, paddles and poles would then follow these.

I can't pretend that this would be easy to arrange, but I believe authenticity would be essential. This would mean getting descendants of the original rowers to come in costumes of their period, and in replica boats. There would have to be a measure of guesswork with regard to Early Man. My previous suggestion as to how rowing, or rather punting began would not be easy to replicate. When it comes to the Celts, however, we have a lot of them still with us in Wales, Scotland, Ireland and Cornwall. It would be easy for them to take part, no passports (unless by then Scotland has become independent), and no travel problems for participants to get to the Regatta, unless there were rail strikes, or hold ups on the M1, M4, M5 or M6. Those from Wales could bring their Coracles.

However, arrangements may be more complicated for participants from Europe or Scandinavia. Firstly, the practical logistics: They could row over the Channel or North Sea as their forefathers did. This would, however, be dangerous and difficult, as well as involving complex boatbuilding. The alternative would be to arrange for replicas of their boats to be either built in this country or brought over by ferry or through the Channel Tunnel. It would bit difficult to get a Roman or Norman Galley or Viking Longboat into an aircraft.

Assuming the boats and crews arrived separately, there would still be logistical challenges including Customs clearance for a considerable number of individuals dressed as armed warriors, with attendant slaves. Short term permits would be necessary (unlike for their ancestors) and they would need to be separated from their weapons during transit.

One can imagine a certain amount of confusion at airports:

No doubt all these difficulties could be overcome, and we would play host to a large number of people of many nations, dressed in the costumes appropriate to what they represent. Everyone likes dressing up for pageants, not least us Brits.

One can imagine the following announcement at Heathrow, or any UK airport:

"WOULD ARRIVALS FROM ROME, SCANDINAVIA, OR NORMANDY, PARTICIPATING IN THE FESTIVAL OF ROWING, PLEASE PROCEED TO THE BAGGAGE HALL TO COLLECT THEIR WEAPONS."

Let us now focus on the Festival itself. I have already proposed events throughout the land, so let's consider the Grand Finale; I have suggested the River Thames for the location, but there may be other suitable rivers. In my opinion they would need to meet the following conditions:

1. Be wide enough, but not too wide, so that cheering crowds on both banks can see the participants.
2. Be deep enough and with enough current to keep things moving swiftly.
3. Have a bridge suitable to accommodate a Royal Party to take the salute from all passing beneath.
4. Have sufficient space to allow for essential music, preferably near the Royal Bridge. I would like this to be as international as possible. Maybe the Berlin Philharmonic Orchestra playing Handel's Water Music, Scottish Pipers performing The Skye Boat Song, a Gospel Choir singing Michael Row the Boat

Ashore. It would certainly have to include a Choir of splendid chaps from our Public schools to sing the Eton Boating Song to remind us of the part played by their elite academies down the years in supporting rowing in the UK.

I want you to picture the scene:

First would come examples of the most ancient rowing craft, reed boats from Egypt, and anywhere else reed boats are, or have been used, dugout canoes, and coracles. Perhaps we could even get examples of the Tibetan and Iraqi coracles. Then, ancient Greek rowing and sail-assisted boats, similar to those used by Jason and the Argonauts and Odysseus. The next group in this historical armada would be the Galleys, Phoenician, Greek, Roman, etc. Replicating these galleys may pose practical challenges, but perhaps someone could design small flat-packs for the occasion.

Following those things, boats from further afield would showcase their rowing and canoeing traditions: Inuit kayaks, American and Canadian First Nation canoes, Polynesian rafts and Māori War canoes. All these would be crewed by people from their respective lands, chanting their original War, rafting or rowing songs as they pass under the bridge on which the Royal Party is placed. I have just realised that the idea of participants singing their native songs clashes with my earlier suggestion of orchestras and choirs on the riverbanks playing near the Royal Pavilion, so perhaps the music providers should perform at a later concert in Hyde Park to conclude the Festival.

The next procession would commemorate the impact of rowing on the history of the UK. Here we would have Celts,

Romans, Saxons, Vikings and Normans, all dressed in authentic clothing or armour, and all clashing their shields and waving their weapons, and trying to look as fierce as our history books would give us to believe they were.

A flotilla of all sorts of boats powered by muscle alone that are still in use throughout the world should come next. Here we could include the Vietnamese foot rowers, Venetian Gondoliers, and lesser-known boats of historic designs still in use. I know from personal experience that dugout canoes are still used on tropical rivers, because I have been a passenger in one (albeit as a tourist) on a river in Sri Lanka. There would have to be a place for the ordinary rowing boat, of course, in this category.

Last of all, we would have to have what are surely the two most iconic teams in present day rowing in this country – Oxford and Cambridge – represented.

There would, of course, have to be a lot of careful thinking given in order to get this right. No doubt both Universities could be very touchy about several issues:

1. Which boat should be first if, as is most likely, the bridge with the Royal Party on it is too narrow to allow them to go through side by side? The possibility of them racing to see who gets there first would go against the principles of the regatta, and in any case could lead to a collision, with resulting tangle of. boats, oars and bodies.

2. Should only boats crewed by men take part, on the grounds that historically the Boat Race was an all-male affair? In this day and age the ladies would not accept this, since the girls also have their inter-varsity

race. A possible solution could be to have two boats for each University, one with an all-male crew, and one with an all-female crew. That, of course, does not resolve the question of who goes through first. Would the gentlemen be gentlemen and let the ladies go first?

Perhaps the best answer to this dilemma would be to have just one boat, crewed by two Oxford men, two Oxford ladies, two Cambridge men and two Cambridge ladies.

The seating arrangements for the crew would have to be decided by drawing straws or tossing coins, as would the gender and University of the Cox.

This boat would approach the bridge at speed, and at the last moment the rowers would raise their oars in a salute to the Monarch and assembled dignitaries.

Let us just imagine the commentator describing this emotional final scene of the Great Regatta:

" —-and now into view comes the especially chosen rowing 8 to represent Oxford and Cambridge Universities, and the immense influence they have had on the sport of rowing in this country. This, the Oxbridge boat, crewed by two men and two women from each University, shows how competitiveness can be put aside, when required in the greater interest of the occasion, to illustrate working together for the common purpose. As they swiftly approach the bridge, they raise their oars to salute the King."

"and as we see them glide so smoothly through to the other side…"

If this were to occur a new saying could be introduced into the English language with the same meaning as "don't count your chickens before they are hatched". Only a few people keep or understand chickens these days, so this new saying might be more appropriate; "don't raise your oars until you're clear of the bridge".